My

INSPIRE

HAPPINESS

DREAM BIG

HOWDY PARTNER

GRATEFUL

Make it happen

FAMILY HISTORY

DREAM HOUSE

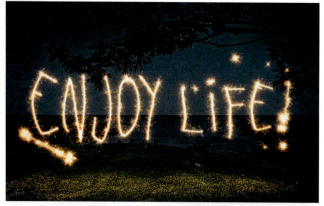

MOVING
FORWARD

FAITH

STEP
BY
STEP

TOGETHER EVERYONE ACHIEVES MORE

GOOD ♥ HEALTH

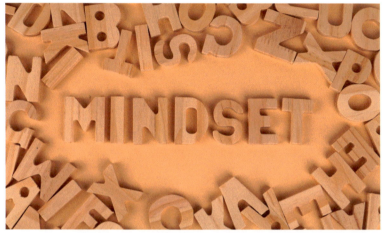

MINDSET

HEALTH FITNESS GOALS

START

Dream Big

TO DO

GOALS

RESPECT

JOY

to be
point of view
Rich
great worth
possessing

APPRECIATE you

MONEY

Grateful!

LOVE IS LOVE

LOVE SONGS

I love you

TOGETHER

forever

WIFE AND HUSBAND

New

home

LOVE

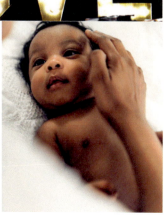

my BEST

SMILE :)

DAD
forever our knight in shining armor

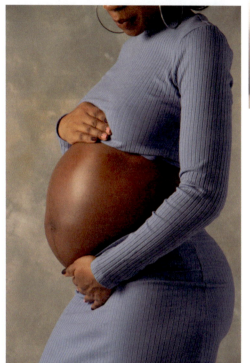

TRUSTED
PARTNER
TRUSTED

BEST
HUSBAND
★ **EVER!** ★

fAmILy

MOM

it's okay to feel your feelings

life is good

♡♡ ♡
BE KIND
to one
ANOTHER

to be best in any rel
point of view.
Encourage
persuade them to
hope or confiden

To Do List

1.

2.

3.

4.

5.

best moment

family

FAITH

HOPE

DO YOUR BEST

FAMILY

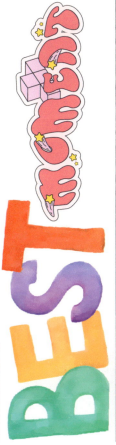

BEST moments

HABITS

BALANCE

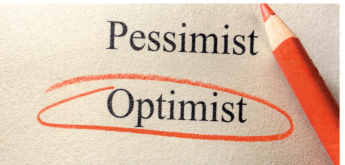

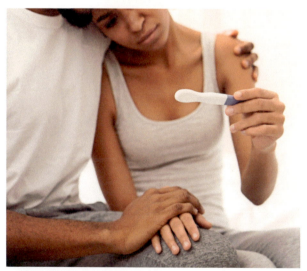

POSITIVE

we

need

to

talk

Loyalty

thankful

HOPE

LOVE

JOY

PEACE

TRAVEL

HONEYMOON

ENGAGEMENT

Thank you

for choosing our Vision Board Clip Art Book

As a special GIFT
I am offering you a
complimentary guide to
download.

This guide is designed to help
you confidently create your
vision board, set SMART
goals, and embrace unlimited
possibilities for your dreams.

Open the camera on your phone
(as if you're going to take a photo)
Hold the phone on the QR CODE below then
a link will appear on your screen
Tap on the link to get your FREE GUIDE

FREE GUIDE

Your Guide to
Creating the Life You
Dream Of

*designed to help you clarify your values, align your beliefs, and set
actionable, meaningful goals that reflect your true self*

Leen W.Hart

Made in the USA
Columbia, SC
01 January 2025

50989534R00029